551.55   20780
Fra··· Fradin, Dennis Brindell

Disaster Tornadoes

Date Due

APR 18	SEP 27 02		
SEP. 0 1			
OCT. 1 6			
ꞏ. 1 0 1997			
OCT 0 1 1997			
APR. 20 1999			
APR 2 1 1999			
SEP. 1 5 1999	FEB 17 00		
APR. 03 2000	APR 27 '04		
OCT. 2 4 2000			
OCT 1 0 2000	FEB 1 '07		

DISASTER!
TORNADOES

By Dennis Brindell Fradin

Consultant: Harry Volkman, Meteorologist

 CHILDRENS PRESS, CHICAGO

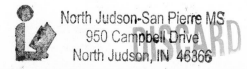

*This tornado was about to strike Union City, Oklahoma
on May 24, 1973.*

For their help, the author thanks:

Frederick P. Ostby, Director, National Severe Storms Forecast Center
Billie Fisher and Josephine Stayton, librarians for
* the Times Publishing Company, Wichita Falls, Texas*
Joyce Ashley, Family Life Editor, The Vernon Daily Record
Tony Stevens, reporter, The Southern Illinoisan
Dave Larzelere, Head Librarian, The Flint Journal
Brian Heckman, National Earth Satellite Service

For my daughter, Diana Judith Fradin

Library of Congress Cataloging in Publication Data
Fradin, Dennis B.
  Tornadoes.
  (Disaster!)
  Summary: Discusses how tornadoes are formed,
how they kill and destroy, and how to predict
and prepare for them. Also describes some
famous tornadoes, including the ones that
struck Vernon and Wichita Falls, Texas, in
April, 1979.
  1. Tornadoes—Juvenile literature.
2. United States—Tornadoes—Juvenile
literature. [1. Tornadoes. 2. Texas—
Tornadoes] I. Title. II. Series: Fradin,
Dennis B.   Disaster!
QC955.F7   551.5′53   81-12277
ISBN 0-516-00854-4   AACR2

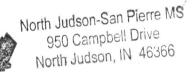

TABLE OF CONTENTS

This satellite image taken at 5:00 P.M. on April 10, 1979 shows that the violent thunderstorms which had spawned the deadly Vernon, Texas twister were now rapidly approaching Wichita Falls, Texas (asterisk). At approximately 6:00 P.M. a monstrous, three-funnel tornado struck Wichita Falls.

1/WHIRLWIND OUTBREAK-1979

At three-thirty on the afternoon of April 10, 1979, the tornado sirens in Vernon, Texas were sounded. The townspeople knew this meant that a tornado had been seen nearby. Many rushed down into their storm cellars or basements. People without cellars hid inside closets or bathrooms. A few ignored the sirens. They had been set off before without a tornado actually striking the town. But this time was different. A huge tornado had already slammed into the outskirts of Vernon.

The tornado was so large and so low to the ground that witnesses couldn't even see a funnel cloud. "The sky turned totally black—I couldn't see anything at all," Suzy Thomas later said. Like many other young people, fourteen-year-old Suzy had just come home from school. She made it down into her cellar just before the twister struck. "I heard a roar—like a train going overhead," she said. Except for the cellar where she was hiding, Suzy's house was completely wrecked by the tornado.

At about the same time that Suzy Thomas's house was destroyed, second-grade teacher Virginia Streit was driving home. Her car was lifted into the air by the tornado. It spun around a number of times and then dropped to the ground. Amazingly, Mrs. Streit survived.

Some people in Vernon weren't so lucky. Eleven were killed. Sixty were injured. More than a hundred homes were damaged or destroyed.

About two and a half hours later, the tornado sirens were sounded in Wichita Falls, Texas—fifty miles from Vernon. People watching television a few minutes after six that evening heard the following bulletin:

THE NATIONAL WEATHER SERVICE HAS ISSUED A TORNADO WARNING EFFECTIVE UNTIL 7 P.M. CENTRAL STANDARD TIME FOR WICHITA COUNTY OF TEXAS AND THE CITY OF WICHITA FALLS, TEXAS. AT 5:58 P.M. RADAR INDICATED A TORNADO TEN MILES SOUTHWEST OF WICHITA FALLS, TEXAS. AT 6 P.M. A SPOTTER REPORTED A TORNADO FIVE MILES SOUTHWEST OF THE WICHITA FALLS MEMORIAL STADIUM ON SOUTHWEST PARKWAY AND MOVING UP TO THE NORTHEAST AT 30 MILES AN HOUR. PERSONS IN THE CITY OF WICHITA FALLS SHOULD TAKE COVER IMMEDIATELY.

Just after this tornado warning was given, television sets in Wichita Falls went black. The tornado had knocked out the city's electrical power. But thanks to the sirens and the television and radio warnings, most people in Wichita Falls had taken cover.

The tornado that struck Wichita Falls was monstrous. Eyewitnesses said that three separate funnels had joined to form one huge tornado. The twister was a half-mile wide. Its winds whirled with speeds that may have reached three hundred miles per hour.

"It reminded me of a freight train when it hit—the way it slammed into our house," Emogene Hall said later. Emogene and William Hall and their sixteen-year-old daughter Allison had hidden inside a closet. "I could hear things flying around and glass shattering. I could feel it when our roof was sucked away." Except for the closet where they had hidden, the Halls' house was destroyed.

The Wichita Falls tornado knocked down buildings as if they were toys. It sent cars flying hundreds of feet through

Above: The three separate funnels of the Wichita Falls
   tornado were about to merge to form one huge tornado.
Below: Wreckage in Vernon, where more than a hundred
   homes were damaged or destroyed by the tornado

*Wichita Falls (above) looked as if it had been hit by a
hydrogen bomb. The tornado left a ten-mile path of wreckage.*

the air before dropping them. It lifted pieces of houses and furniture a half-mile into the sky. The whirling winds smashed glass and sent it flying.

As the tornado struck, men at the Wichita Falls National Guard Armory were preparing to head for Vernon. They were planning to help that tornado-stricken city. The tornado destroyed the armory, but the sixty men survived by hiding in a vault. At a Wichita Falls restaurant, the manager yelled for people to run to the back of the building. Seconds later, the tornado struck. The twister lifted the restaurant's roof and then slammed it back down, crushing the walls. Three people in the restaurant were killed by falling debris.

After the tornado was finished with Wichita Falls, Texas, the city looked as if it had been hit by a hydrogen bomb. Section of buildings, broken furniture, and smashed cars lay scattered on a ten-mile-long path. Forty-six people in Wichita Falls were dead. Hundreds were injured. Twenty thousand of the city's hundred thousand people were homeless.

On that one day—April 10, 1979—ten tornadoes touched down in Texas and Oklahoma. Sixty-two people died in the twisters.

Considering the damage that had been done, it was amazing that the death toll was so low. The tornado sirens and the television and radio warnings saved many people. Wichita Falls newspapers estimated that without those warnings hundreds, or even thousands, might have died.

Almost immediately, people in Wichita Falls and the other tornado-torn cities began rescue and relief operations. Volunteers and city workers dug people out of the wreckage. Some of them were still alive. Hospital staffs worked frantically to save the lives of the injured. Many people donated blood. Neighbors helped each other clear debris and

Wichita Falls tornado victims kept their sense of humor.

salvage valuable items from homes. There were even touches of humor. People put up signs that said GONE WITH THE WIND and WE'RE OFF TO SEE THE WIZARD on sites where their homes and offices once had stood.

The Red Cross and the Salvation Army set up emergency centers in Wichita Falls and Vernon. They provided the homeless with food, clothing, and shelter. Soon the United States government brought in mobile homes to provide temporary housing.

It would take a long time to rebuild what the tornadoes had destroyed in minutes. Even two years later, some of the homes, offices, and churches were not yet rebuilt. Foundations marked sites where houses once had stood. Those who lived through it would remember "Terrible Tuesday" for the rest of their lives.

2/SURVIVORS-TEXAS, 1979

What is a tornado like? Those who have lived through one can best answer that. Here are the stories of some survivors of the April 10, 1979 tornadoes:

Billy Joe and Bryan Nava - Vernon, Texas

"It was thundering and lightning when we left school on the school bus," twelve-year-old Billy Joe Nava recalled two years later. "When we got home, my brother Jason wanted to go inside the house and watch cartoons. But my Aunt Peggy next door told us to go down into their storm cellar."

A storm cellar is an underground hiding place built separately from the house. When tornado sirens sound, people without basements often head to the nearest storm cellar. Many people keep blankets, transistor radios, candles, water, and first-aid supplies in their storm cellars.

While Billy Joe Nava and his three brothers were in the storm cellar with other members of their family, the tornado struck. "We couldn't close the door of the storm cellar because of the wind," he remembers. "Then the tornado went by and the door busted right off."

Billy Joe and his relatives stayed in the storm cellar for about ten minutes. When they were sure that the twister had passed, they came out. "My room was the only part of our house that was still there," Billy Joe said. "Our street looked like something you see in a war movie. Everything looked as if it had been bombed."

"For a long time after the tornado I'd get real scared just if it started to get cloudy," Billy Joe's ten-year-old brother

Bryan said. "I had nightmares about it. I kept thinking another tornado would come."

"Me, too," said Billy Joe. "But our daddy taught us not to get scared. He showed us the difference between regular clouds and ones that might have tornadoes. We also made a plan. No matter where we are, we have some place in mind to go if the tornado sirens go off."

Billy Nava - Vernon, Texas

As the tornado approached Vernon, thirty-three-year-old Billy Nava and his brother Kenneth raced toward their homes in a pickup truck. The two brothers lived next door to each other. Billy and his wife had four children. Kenneth and his wife also had four. The brothers were very worried about their families. They didn't know that everyone was safely inside the storm cellar in Kenneth Nava's backyard.

Just as Billy drove the pickup into his driveway, the tornado struck.

"It hit the pickup and sucked every window out of it," Nava remembered two years later. "I looked down and it looked as if a stick of dynamite had hit my brother's house. The roof was gone." Billy was looking *down* because, for a few seconds, the tornado had lifted the pickup truck about twenty-five feet off the ground.

"The tornado set us down in what had been my brother's living room," Billy continued. "We were headed the other way from where we'd been facing."

Seeing no sign of anyone in the ruins of their houses, the brothers raced to the storm cellar in Kenneth Nava's yard. They were relieved to find their families safe.

12

While in the air, Billy was struck in the head. With a rag tied around the bleeding gash, Billy set out with his brother to check on their neighbors.

Billy soon found the bodies of Donna Shelton and her three-year-old daughter, Luann.

Billy and Kenneth Nava also found several living people. "A block from our houses we heard someone screaming for help," Billy said. "We didn't know who it was. We couldn't even tell whose house it was because the houses were so totally wrecked there was no way to tell one from the other. My brother and I lifted a wall away and rescued a teenage girl." The girl was sixteen-year-old Tracee Cerda. She had to be rushed to the hospital, where her spleen was removed.

Billy Nava worked late into the night before going to the hospital to have his own wounds tended. His head wound required about eight stitches. Something—he never knew what—had punctured one side of his arm and come out the other. The arm, too, needed stitches.

"But what hurt worst was the glass," he remembered. "The wind had blown glass, splinters, wood, and dust into my back like a blast from a shotgun. My wife picked it out of my back for a week.

"Before the tornado struck Vernon, a lot of people used to ignore the sirens," said Billy Nava. "In fact, some used to go out and look up at the clouds. It's different now. Whenever the sirens blow everyone goes down into the cellar."

Tracee Cerda · Vernon, Texas

Two years after the Vernon tornado, Tracee Cerda still trembled whenever she saw storm clouds or heard the tornado sirens. Tracee had survived the tornado. But it broke three of her ribs and ruptured her spleen.

"I had just gotten home from school and was watching TV," eighteen-year-old Tracee remembered. "Suddenly the electricity in the house went off. I looked out the window but I couldn't see a thing, so I went to the door and opened it. All I saw was solid black. And then the wind blew the door right off its hinges."

Although the sirens hadn't yet blown when the tornado struck Tracee's part of town, the great wind was enough to send her running toward her bedroom. Tracee got part-way under her bed. "Then I heard a roar that sounded like a train going right over our house. For a while it felt like the bed was being lifted right up and I could see clothes and glass flying all over my room. Then the bed and part of a wall came down real hard on top of me and I was trapped."

Tracee dug away some of the bricks so that she could breathe. But she couldn't pull herself out from under the debris.

Her calls for help were heard by Billy and Kenneth Nava, the two brothers who had just come home to check on their own families. "Kenneth and Billy probably saved my life," Tracee said. "They pulled the bricks off me and carried me away. When they picked me up I really started to hurt. Before that I had been too scared to hurt."

Tracee was taken to the hospital, where she was operated on right away. Her spleen was ruptured and had to be removed. Three of her ribs were broken. She spent two weeks in the hospital. Then she went to live at the house of some friends while her parents' house was rebuilt. Sixteen months after the tornado, Tracee was married. She now lives in another part of Vernon.

"Afterward, people asked me why I didn't hide in the bathtub instead of under the bed. It's lucky I picked the bed. The bathtub was blown out of our house and hasn't been found yet.

"The tornado was the worst experience in my life—by far," Tracee Cerda said. "I still have nightmares about it. I hope nothing else in my life will ever be that bad."

The Hall Family - Wichita Falls, Texas

"Everybody should have a hiding place in mind long before a tornado strikes," said Dr. William Hall two years after the big one struck Wichita Falls.

Long before "Terrible Tuesday," Dr. Hall had a hiding place in mind. Since his house didn't have a basement, he figured that a closet inside an interior bedroom would be best.

A Wichita Falls dentist, Dr. Hall had just gotten home from work when the tornado approached the city. "A bulletin on TV said that a tornado had touched down about five miles southwest of here. I wasn't too concerned. I just kept reading the paper and listening to the TV. About a minute later, the TV blacked out and we heard the sirens.

The Hall family of Wichita Falls

*The Halls' neighborhood (above) looked like
a war zone after the tornado had struck.*

"My daughter Allison and I went outside and looked toward the southwest and there was this big black cloud. We could see big objects blowing in it way up high in the sky."

Dr. Hall ran into the kitchen where his wife, Emogene, was preparing dinner. He tried to get his wife and daughter to go into the closet, but they wanted to run to the car and drive away. Finally, Dr. Hall grabbed them and pulled them into the closet. On the way, he also grabbed some pillows from the couch to shield their heads.

"Even if we hadn't heard the sirens or seen the tornado, we would have known that something was about to happen," continued eighteen-year-old Allison Hall. "It got real quiet and still. It was very hard to breathe and I felt that I was going to suffocate. By the time Daddy took us into the closet I was crying and yelling and screaming. Then when I heard this loud noise like a train hitting our house I thought we were going to die."

"I wasn't scared until it hit; then I really panicked," continued her mother, Emogene Hall. "I could hear stuff flying all over the place and glass shattering. The tornado also

The tornado smashed the Halls' house and wrecked the cars in the driveway (above).

had this horrible musty smell from all the debris it was carrying. My ears were stopped up and it felt like my head would explode outward."

Except for the closet where they were hiding, the Halls' house was completely smashed. Once he saw that Mrs. Hall and Allison were all right, Dr. Hall wanted to check on his mother, who lived nearby. His cars were wrecked, so he borrowed a car and drove toward his mother's house.

"It looked like a war zone on the streets," Dr. Hall remembered. "There were disintegrated houses and electrical wires all over the place. There were people lying in ditches next to overturned cars and cars that were on fire."

Although Dr. Hall's mother was not badly injured, her house was completely wrecked. So were Dr. Hall's dental office and the Halls' church. All of the important buildings in their lives were demolished. But the Halls were thankful that they had survived.

"My main advice to people is to plan ahead in case of a tornado," said Dr. Hall. "It takes so little time to think of the safest place and it can save your life."

Dennis Spruill,
city editor of the
Wichita Falls Times.

Dennis Spruill - Wichita Falls, Texas

"My neighbor and I were standing on his pickup truck watching this gray cloud approach," remembered Dennis Spruill, city editor of the *Wichita Falls Times.* "I thought it couldn't be a tornado because it was too big. As it moved toward me it turned from light gray to dark gray to black. Then I could make out the most monstrous funnel I've ever seen."

Spruill's first impulse was to get in his car and drive away. "Then I thought, no, they tell you not to get in a car. I decided to do what the experts recommend. I went back inside the house and tried to determine the safest place."

Once inside, Spruill glanced at the television he had been watching for weather bulletins. "There was a warning to get in the house and take cover. The announcer started to say something else but the TV went black. Later I found out that one of the first things that the tornado hit was the city's main power trunk."

Spruill and his dog were alone in the house. Luckily, his two children were in Oklahoma with their grandparents. His wife was at the bank where she worked.

Spruill decided that the bathroom was the safest place in the house. "I squeezed myself between the toilet and the tub and stuffed my dog under my chest to protect her. Then I heard

18

the tornado. It reminded me of a powerful generator, like the turbines in a nuclear plant.''

First, Spruill felt his house begin to shake. ''Then I heard the front of my house go—it sounded like an explosion as the wood ripped. There were boards and shingles from the roof flying around like arrows. Suddenly it felt very cool, so I glanced up. The roof was gone.''

Although debris was flying past his head, Dennis Spruill had an even greater worry. ''I could feel the tornado pulling my hair and my clothes upward. I could feel it tugging on me. I grabbed the toilet and held on for dear life because I felt that the tornado was about to suck me out of the room.''

Spruill managed to hold on until the tornado passed. For about five minutes he lay covered by boards and other debris. Then he climbed out from under the junk. He saw that the tornado had destroyed his entire house—except for the bathroom where he and the dog had hidden.

Spruill started to walk toward the bank to check on his wife. ''As far as I could see there were wrecked homes, turned-over cars, and downed power lines. I stepped over the electrical lines until I realized that the power was out.

''The drive-in window where my wife worked was completely destroyed. The rest of the bank was a pile of rubble. There was nothing to distinguish that it had ever been a building at all.'' Fortunately, however, Jeanette Spruill and other bank employees had hidden in the bank's safest place— the money vault.

''The warning sirens and the warnings on TV saved many lives—perhaps mine and my wife's,'' Dennis Spruill said. ''Some people didn't pay attention to the warnings and died for it. Some also tried to flee and many of them wound up in the graveyard. My wife and I did what the experts advised and we lived through it.''

When a tornado touches down, it sweeps up debris from the ground. In the distance, roof shingles and tree branches can be seen swirling high inside the twister (above).

3/THE SCIENCE OF TORNADOES

Late on a spring afternoon, thunderstorms form across much of the United States. Rain begins to fall and huge chunks of hail smack down from the sky. Suddenly a gray whirling funnel dips down from a big storm cloud. People shout "Tornado!" and sirens go off to warn those who haven't seen it. When the tornado touches down, its color darkens because of the debris it is sweeping up from the ground. In the distance, roof shingles and tree branches can be seen swirling high inside the twister. When the tornado is a few miles away, it sounds like the hum of a trillion bees. But as it approaches, the sound is more like the roar of a hundred freight trains. By this time, however, everyone in its path should be hiding in a basement or another safe place. The tornado is capable of tearing up a house and killing people.

This tornado was photographed near Enid, Oklahoma on June 5, 1966.

Although tornadoes form in many parts of the world, the United States is hit by almost all of the severe ones. According to meteorologists (weather scientists), about seven hundred tornadoes touch down each year in the United States. On an average, about a hundred Americans per year are killed by tornadoes. Tornadoes rank as the nation's second-deadliest type of natural disaster. In the past thirty years, only floods have killed more Americans.

Tornadoes have been seen in all fifty states. But the midwestern and southcentral states are hit hardest. This area—roughly down the middle of the country—is sometimes called "Tornado Alley."

Tornadoes and How They Work

A tornado is a violently whirling column of air that descends from a thundercloud system and touches the ground. Because tornadoes twist and turn as they move, many people call them "twisters." The word tornado itself comes from the Latin word *tornare,* which means "to turn."

Tornadoes are sometimes called the "little sisters" of hurricanes, which are also windstorms that whirl in a circular motion. Hurricanes are much bigger. But the winds in tornadoes are much stronger. In fact, tornadoes are by far the strongest windstorms on our planet.

If you've ever been out in a thirty-mile-per-hour wind, you know that the gusts can nearly knock you down. Such a wind is nothing compared to a tornado. The wind speed inside a tornado can reach three hundred miles per hour or more.

Fortunately, tornadoes aren't very big. Although a 1974 tornado near Stamping Ground, Kentucky cut a path that was

A tornado is a violently whirling column of air that descends
from a thundercloud system and touches the ground. As it moves
along the ground, it destroys everything in its path.
Tornadoes are the most destructive of all storms on earth.

Trees broken off by a tornado whirled with the winds to create paths like tire tracks in this plowed field in Monroe, Wisconsin in 1965.

A 1953 tornado cut a path through the north side of the historic Mississippi River town of Vicksburg, Mississippi (above).

five miles wide, most tornadoes are a quarter of a mile wide or less. Tornadoes don't last very long, either. Their average time on the ground is only about ten minutes. They generally travel for only about fifteen miles before fizzling out.

Although the winds inside a tornado reach great speeds, the tornado itself usually moves forward at about thirty miles per hour. People have outdriven tornadoes. But because tornadoes often change their paths, it would be foolish to leave a building and try to flee from one by car. Tornadoes have been known to make figure 8s, zig-zags, and U-turns. They have even been known to stand still for more than fifteen minutes. So people who try to flee from tornadoes in cars sometimes find themselves heading right *toward* the funnel.

In the United States, the winds in a tornado usually turn in a counterclockwise direction. This means that they move in the opposite direction from the hands of a clock. Tornadoes in the United States usually come from the southwest, west, or south. But they have been known to come from other directions.

This Enid, Oklahoma funnel cloud resembles the trunk of a tree.

From a distance, tornadoes often look like funnels. Their
appearance also has been compared to a water hose, an
elephant's trunk, a rope, a mushroom's stem, and a tree
trunk. The biggest tornadoes sometimes appear to be great,
black walls of clouds. That is because they are so big and so
close to the ground that people can't make out a shape.

Twisters take on the color of the things they've sucked up.
A tornado that passes over a field of brown dirt will look
brown in the sky. Tornadoes have turned solid white while
churning up fields of snow. Tornadoes can fill themselves
with water, too, by sucking up parts of lakes or oceans.
Tornadoes that touch down over lakes or oceans are called
waterspouts.

Most people who have seen tornadoes have viewed them
from a distance. Few have ever looked directly up into a

Tornadoes that touch down on lakes or oceans are called
waterspouts because they suck up water into their swirling winds.

tornado's funnel and lived to tell about it. But this is what the inside, or *vortex,* of one tornado looked like to Will Keller, a farmer who lived near Greensburg, Kansas:

It was on the afternoon of June 22, 1928, between 3 and 4 o'clock. I was out in my field with my family looking over the ruins of our wheat crop which had just been completely destroyed by a hailstorm. ı noticed an umbrella-shaped cloud in the west and southwest. . . . hanging from the greenish-black base of the cloud was not just *one* tornado, but *three.*

One of the tornadoes was already perilously near and apparently headed directly for our place. I lost no time therefore in hurrying with my family to our cyclone cellar.

The family had entered the cellar and I was in the doorway just about to enter and close the door when I decided that I would take a last look at the approaching tornado. . . . Two of the tornadoes were some distance away and looked to me like great ropes dangling from the clouds, but the near one was shaped more like a funnel with ragged clouds surrounding it. It appeared to be much larger and more energetic than the others and it occupied the central position of the cloud. . . . I knew that if the tornado again dipped I could drop down and close the door before any harm could be done. . . . At last the great shaggy end of the funnel hung directly overhead. Everything was as still as death. There was a strong gassy odor and it seemed that I could not breathe. There was a screaming hissing sound coming directly from the end of the funnel. I looked up and to my astonishment I saw right up into the heart of the tornado. There was a circular opening in the center of the funnel, about 50 or 100 feet in diameter, and extending straight upward for a distance of at least one half mile, as best I could judge under the circumstances. The walls of this opening were of rotating clouds and the whole was made brilliantly visible by constant flashes of lightning which zigzagged from side to side. Had it not been for the lightning I could not have seen the opening, not any distance up into it anyway. . . .

You may have wondered about the loud noises people have heard in tornadoes. If you whirl something in a circle, you can hear noise made by the wind. With their tremendous winds, tornadoes make a lot of noise. It is also believed that thunder inside tornadoes adds to the noise.

How Tornadoes Are Formed

Scientists have long known the general conditions that create tornadoes. They occur when warm, moist air from the south meets cold, dry air moving down from the north. Violent weather is created at the *front,* or border, of these two kinds of air. Thunderstorms are formed there. So are tornadoes.

A kind of civil war in the sky occurs as the warm southern air meets the cold northern air. Cold air is heavier than warm air so it pushes beneath the warm air. The warm air is forced to rise quickly. In places, the two bodies of air battling each other begin to rotate. The rotating winds become a tornado.

Exactly how this happens is not yet known. Scientists have many different theories to explain the tornado-forming processes. They agree that many complex factors are involved. The earth's spin and the jet stream (fast-moving winds high above the ground) are two of the factors that create the spinning funnel cloud.

Although scientists may not know exactly how tornadoes are born, they can easily spot conditions that make them likely. When meteorologists see cold air about to clash with warm air, they know that tornadoes may develop.

They also know when to watch most closely for tornadoes. Most tornadoes occur in April, May, and June. During those months, very warm air often moves up through the southern United States from the Gulf of Mexico. During those same months, there is still much cold air coming down from Canada.

On a day when the warm air meets the cold air, there can be many tornadoes. When a large number of tornadoes form in a certain area, meteorologists call it a "tornado outbreak."

In the United States, violent thunderstorms and tornadoes frequently develop when warm, moist air from the Gulf of Mexico rises to meet cold, dry air coming down from Canada. Most tornadoes occur within "Tornado Alley"—a wide north-south band roughly in the middle of the country.

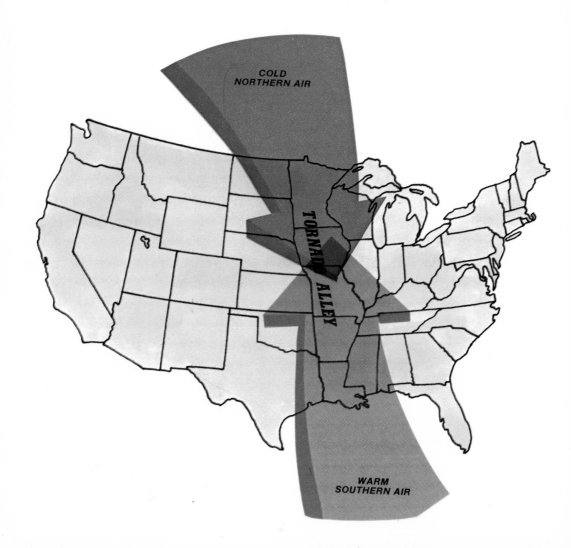

The deadly power of this tornado sucked up the roof of the Fresno, California Air Terminal in February, 1980.

How Tornadoes Kill and Destroy

The three-hundred-mile-per-hour winds of a tornado are the main cause of death and destruction. Roofs and walls are torn apart by the winds. As the buildings collapse, people are killed. The fierce winds can also snatch people out of their houses and send them flying into streets and fields.

The winds also send small objects flying with the force of machine-gun fire. Glass, rocks, and boards fly at incredible speeds, sometimes killing people in their paths.

The sucking power of a tornado is deadly, too. Like a titanic vacuum cleaner, it sucks up roofs, trees, cars, animals, and human beings. These objects are lifted high into the air and then slammed to the ground.

Numb with shock and disbelief, these tornado victims stare at the wreckage of their homes.

A victim of the Oak Lawn, Illinois tornado of April 22, 1967 takes inventory in the kitchen of her home, which was almost completely destroyed.

There is another way tornadoes kill and destroy. Have you ever blown up a balloon until it popped? The balloon bursts because the pressure inside it becomes greater than the pressure outside. The air pressure of a tornado is very low, because the rapid spinning of its winds pulls air away from its center. As a tornado passes over a building, the pressure inside the building is much greater than the pressure of the tornado. So, like the balloon, buildings sometimes explode outward. A tornado's low air pressure sometimes makes it hard for people to breathe and gives them the feeling that their heads are about to explode.

There are less-direct ways that tornadoes do lasting harm to people. By leaving people homeless, tornadoes totally disrupt their lives. Tornadoes also can give people the scare of their lives. In Vernon, Texas, seventy-three-year-old Loyd Stamps and his seventy-two-year-old wife Anna Mae were both away from home when the tornado struck. But Mrs. Stamps thought that her husband had been at home. Upon seeing the rubble of their house, Mrs. Stamps became so worried about him that she had a stroke, which crippled a leg and an arm. She won't show up in the statistics of injured people. Yet the tornado hurt her just as surely as if it had struck her directly.

33

4/SOME MAJOR TORNADOES

American Indians must have sighted tornadoes long ago. But the first written description of a tornado in America was made by an Englishman in 1586. The year before, the English had formed their first colony in America—the Roanoke Colony—in what is now North Carolina. Colonist Ralph Lane spotted some waterspouts at sea in June of 1586. In his diary he wrote: "We had thunder and rain with hailstones as big as hen's eggs. There were great spouts at the seas as though heaven and earth would have met."

Since then, many thousands of tornadoes have touched down in America. The following are descriptions of just a few of the best-known tornadoes and tornado outbreaks:

Great Natchez, Mississippi - May 7, 1840

Natchez, Mississippi is the oldest town on the Mississippi River. It was founded by the French in 1716. By the early 1800s, many wealthy American cotton planters lived in Natchez. It was a city of huge mansions and lovely gardens.

At 12:45 on the afternoon of May 7, 1840, thunder could be heard rumbling southwest of Natchez. Natchez weather scientist Henry Tooley kept a careful account of what happened. He wrote that by 1:45 in the afternoon "a blackness of darkness overspread the heavens." The only light in the sky came from the flashes of lightning, and the thunder "shook the solid earth." At 2:00 a large tornado struck Natchez.

Trees along the Mississippi River were uprooted by the tornado. Flatboats and steamboats sank. As the lightning flashed, people saw roofs, chimneys, and other debris whirling high in the sky.

Brick houses were torn to bits. Two churches and the Natchez theater were wrecked. Hotels were destroyed. Many people were trapped under the wrecked buildings.

After the tornado passed, the people of Natchez began to dig through the ruins. "We are all in confusion, and surrounded by the destitute and houseless, the wounded and the dying," a Natchez newspaper reported. "Our beautiful city is shattered as if it had been stormed by all the cannon of Austerlitz." Several people were dug out of the ruins after being buried for hours. Many others weren't so lucky. More than three hundred people died, making this the nation's worst tornado disaster in the years before the Civil War.

Tri-State - 1925

On Wednesday, March 18, 1925, a storm swept into the midwestern United States. At the time, people were at work in offices and factories. Children were at school. As the storm approached, few persons sought shelter. Storms are common in the Midwest during March. This storm was unusual, however. Accompanying it was the most deadly tornado ever to strike the United States.

The tornado was so large and so close to the ground that it appeared only as a dark, low cloud. No one saw a funnel. The tornado first touched down in Reynolds County, Missouri at one o'clock in the afternoon. Trees were torn out by their roots. Houses were sucked up by the tornado and then strewn about like sticks. About twenty-five people were killed in southeastern Missouri. But this was only the beginning.

The Tri-State Tornado of 1925 caused tremendous damage in Missouri, Illinois, and Indiana (above). The death toll of 689 made this tornado the most deadly ever to strike the United States.

Most tornadoes stay on the ground for about 15 miles before fizzling out. This tornado traveled along the ground for 219 miles—an all-time record. Just about everything in its path was smashed to smithereens.

From Missouri, the huge black cloud whirled into Illinois. It gouged a mile-wide path of death and destruction along the southern tip of the state. Murphysboro, Illinois was the hardest-hit town in the tornado's path. More than two hundred Murphysboro people were killed. Three-quarters of the town was destroyed.

In the nearby town of De Soto, F.M. Hewitt watched the huge cloud approach. Hewitt later said that he heard a loud roar coming from inside the cloud. He watched in disbelief as a house was blown apart by the oncoming tornado. Moments later he sought shelter inside another house. It, too, was blown to bits. Hewitt found himself blown safely out onto the street.

More than a hundred others in De Soto did not survive. At a leveled school, twenty students and all three teachers were killed.

The tornado showed its power in other ways besides flattening buildings. Cars were sucked up by the tornado, carried through the air for hundreds of feet, and then dropped. Some drivers were sucked right out of the cars and thrown onto the road. At Murphysboro, eleven huge locomotives were wrecked. Near West Frankfort, Illinois, miners were underground in the New Orient mine when the tornado passed. The miners heard its roar and felt the shock of it hitting the ground.

After sweeping across southern Illinois, the tornado entered Indiana. At the little town of Griffin, every single building was knocked down. Fifty people were killed in that one town.

The tornado finally fizzled out over Indiana. Because it had gone through three states—Missouri, Illinois, and Indiana—it was called the Tri-State Tornado. In all, the Tri-State Tornado killed 689 people—still the record number of deaths in a single tornado. That huge death toll made it one of the worst natural disasters ever to strike the United States. The tornado also injured more than 2,000 persons. Houses, churches, factories, schools, and farms lay strewn along its 219-mile path. Four towns no longer existed. They had been blown to bits.

If a tornado like that one struck today, it would cause great destruction. Probably, though, there would be fewer deaths. The government now has warning systems so that people can go to a safe place before a tornado strikes.

Operation Tornado - Flint, Michigan, 1953

The year 1953 was a big one for tornadoes. On May 11 of that year more than a hundred people were killed by a single twister in Texas. Then, between June 7 and June 9, 234 people died in a tornado flurry that struck New England, Michigan, and Ohio.

One of the deadliest tornadoes of 1953—or any other year—hit the city of Flint, Michigan on June 8, 1953. The sky turned green, a huge funnel dipped down, and in minutes 116 people in the car-making city were dead. More than 900 were injured. Hundreds were homeless.

Back in America's early years, the pioneers had "house-raisings." Neighbors helped newcomers build their homes. In the summer of 1953, the people of Flint decided to have house-raisings for those whose homes had been destroyed. Churches, businesses, and the Flint city government asked for volunteers. They planned a big "building bee" called "Operation Tornado."

The Flint, Michigan tornado of 1953 (below) killed 116 people.

This house-raising in Flint took place during "Operation Tornado," one of the largest volunteer building projects in the history of the United States.

Operation Tornado was held on the weekend of August 29-30, 1953. August 29 was very hot. The temperature rose to ninety degrees. But early that morning about four thousand men, women, and children came to the tornado-smashed streets of Flint. The volunteers sawed and hammered. They laid bricks and put down floors. They painted walls and built roofs. By the end of Saturday, roofs were going up over houses that had had only foundations at the start of the day.

The next day—Sunday—even more people came to join the building bee. By Sunday night, 193 houses had been completed or partially built. This was one of the largest volunteer building projects in the history of the United States. Even after Operation Tornado was over, electricians and other volunteers returned to help put finishing touches on the houses.

Usually, it takes many months to rebuild tornado-wrecked homes. Thanks to their neighbors' help, many Flint people were in their new homes by the end of summer.

Super Outbreak-April 3-4, 1974

Picture 148 tornadoes battering our country in an eighteen-hour period. That happened in the spring of 1974. A mass of warm air coming from the Gulf of Mexico met a mass of cold air coming from the west. Tornadoes were formed from Alabama to Ontario, Canada. The barrage began about midday on April third and continued until the morning of the fourth.

These twisters killed 315 people—more than had been killed by tornadoes in the previous three years. Thousands of people were injured. Dozens of towns were smashed.

Xenia, Ohio was one of the the hardest-hit towns. "All you could hear was the wind, the crashes, and the people praying," a Xenia survivor said later. When the tornado had moved out of Xenia, more than 30 townspeople were dead. About 1,000 of the town's 25,000 people were injured. "Fifty percent of Xenia has gone—the houses, the schools, even the trees," said the mayor of the town. The tornado that hit Xenia was so strong that it picked up a tractor-trailer and tossed it onto the roof of a bowling alley. Letters and papers swept out of houses were later found two hundred miles away.

Another deadly twister struck the town of Jasper, Alabama. Jasper's main street was demolished. Its city hall was smashed. A radio announcer watched the tornado strike the police station and then said: "We can't talk to the police department—it just blew away!"

In the state of Indiana, more than fifty people were killed by twisters. At what was once Martinsburg, Indiana, a state trooper reported that the town "just isn't there anymore." It was one of several towns blown off the map. Near Monticello,

Indiana, seventeen-year-old Karen Scott was driving across a bridge when a tornado lifted her van and tossed it into a lake. Karen escaped from the sinking van and swam to safety, but five others in the vehicle died.

There were other amazing stories of survival. In Sugar Valley, Georgia, a twister carried a nine-year-old boy six hundred feet through the air. He survived, although his parents and two sisters did not. In Hillsdale, Michigan, Ballard and Carolyn Holbrook used their own bodies to shield their two children. Mr. and Mrs. Holbrook were killed when the twister struck. The children, lying under them, survived.

By the time the outbreak ended early on the morning of April 4, 148 twisters had struck. Known as the "Super Outbreak," this still holds the record as the biggest tornado barrage in United States history. The more than $600 million in damage holds the record for the most destruction ever caused by a group of tornadoes.

This map shows some of the areas that were hardest hit during the "Super Outbreak" of 1974.

SOME DEADLY TORNADOES AND TORNADO OUTBREAKS IN THE UNITED STATES

Date	Place	Number of Tornadoes	Deaths
May 7, 1840	Natchez, Mississippi	1	More than 300 (the deadliest tornado before the Civil War)
June 3, 1860	Iowa and Illinois	1 (known as the "Camanche Tornado," because it struck Camanche, Iowa)	About 200
February 19, 1884	Alabama, Mississippi, North Carolina, South Carolina, Tennessee, Indiana, Kentucky	60	800
May 27, 1896	St. Louis, Missouri and East St. Louis, Illinois	1	306
May 26-27, 1917	Arkansas, Alabama, Mississippi Illinois, Indiana, Kentucky, Tennessee	Exact number unknown, but thought to be large	249
April 20, 1920	Alabama, Mississippi, Tennessee	6	220
March 18, 1925	Missouri, Illinois, and Indiana	1 (the Tri-State Tornado)	689 (the most ever killed by a single tornado; about 100 other people died in 7 other tornadoes on the same day)
May 8-9, 1927	Texas, Louisiana, Indiana, Michigan, Missouri, Nebraska	36	227
March 21, 1932	Alabama, Mississippi, Tennessee, Georgia	27	321
April 5-6, 1936	Arkansas, Tennessee, Alabama, Georgia, South Carolina	22	498
March 21-22, 1952	Arkansas, Tennessee, Missouri, Kentucky, Alabama, Mississippi	31	343

May 11, 1953	Texas	1	114
June 7-9, 1953	Michigan, Ohio, and New England	12	234
April 11-12, 1965	Indiana, Illinois, Iowa, Wisconsin, Ohio, Michigan	47 (known as the "Palm Sunday Outbreak")	257
April 3-4, 1974	Thirteen different states in the Eastern, Southern, and Midwestern United States, and also a small portion of Canada	148 (the largest outbreak ever recorded)	315
April 10, 1979	Texas and Oklahoma	10	62

This house at Grafton, Ohio was struck by one of the forty-seven tornadoes that were part of the "Palm Sunday Outbreak" of 1965.

Railroad cars and trailer trucks were tossed about like toys during a tornado that touched down in Chicago in 1961.

A 1966 tornado that ripped through Jackson, Mississippi left only the mangled skeleton of this Continental Can Company building.

An entire wall of this St. Louis apartment house was ripped away by a tornado in 1959.

5/TORNADO POWER

After the 1979 tornado in Vernon, Texas, Suzy Thomas's family was missing some important papers. They figured they'd never see those papers again. But the papers were sent back to them. They had been blown by the tornado to Woodward, Oklahoma—more than 150 miles away.

The tornado also uprooted 100-foot-tall trees in the horse pasture outside Suzy Thomas's house. Two years later, the gigantic trees were still scattered throughout the pasture.

Such occurrences happen often during tornadoes. Their powerful winds can do many astounding things.

Cars are often sent flying long distances by tornadoes. So are other heavy objects. In 1975, a Mississippi twister lifted a home freezer and blew it more than a mile through the air before dropping it. In 1931, a Minnesota tornado lifted a train car weighing 160,000 pounds and carried it 80 feet through the air before throwing it in a ditch. Of the 117 people in the train car, only one man died.

Buildings, too, have been moved by tornadoes. A 1966 tornado in Topeka, Kansas moved a ten-story building right off its foundations. Do you remember how Dorothy in *The Wizard of Oz* had her house lifted by a twister? In Ponca City, Oklahoma, a man and his wife were eating supper when their house was suddenly lifted by a tornado. Except for the floor, the house was blown to pieces. The floor—with the man and woman on it—was set back down on the ground. The unhurt couple weren't in the land of Oz, though. They were still in Ponca City, Oklahoma.

Many strange things have happened to animals during tornadoes. Chickens have had all their feathers plucked out by the strong winds. Sheep have had their wool sheared off.

*Sigurd and Louise Hyland and their son Calvin
(left) survived a 1970 tornado that demolished their
home and farm buildings. One of their horses,
Cheyenne Lady (above with her colt Breezy),
was picked up and blown a mile through the air.*

Animals have found themselves going on unexpected trips inside tornadoes. Once in Kansas, a herd of steers was sent flying through the sky. One person who saw them said that they looked "like a flight of gigantic birds."

You've heard the expression "It's raining cats and dogs." Once, frogs actually rained down from the sky. This happened after a tornado sucked up a pond that contained hundreds of frogs. When the pond water was set down, so were the frogs.

During a 1970 tornado in Radcliffe, Iowa, Louise Hyland's horse was picked up and blown a mile through the air. "Cheyenne Lady came down on a fence post that poked a hole in her back," Mrs. Hyland remembers. "But she recovered." During the 1979 tornado in Vernon, Texas, a horse was picked up and blown through the air for about two hundred yards. The horse landed near what had been the kitchen of Juan and Isabel Martinez.

People, too, have been carried through the air by tornadoes. A 1913 Nebraska twister carried a young woman through the air for a quarter of a mile. She landed unharmed. Back in 1899, a young boy was lifted by a tornado with his mother and another woman in Kirksville, Missouri. The twister also picked up a horse. According to witnesses, the horse went over a church steeple. After a flight of several blocks, the three people and the horse were set down on the ground. The boy later said that he had seen the horse while in the air. "At one time it was directly over me," he said, "and I was very much afraid I would come in contact with its flying heels."

After tornadoes have passed, people often find objects driven like spears into other objects. It is common to find straw and grass driven into trees and buildings. After a tornado struck St. Louis in 1896, weather bureau chief Willis Moore found a garden spade driven six inches into a tree limb. Before the tornado struck Vernon, Texas in 1979, the Nava family had a deck of cards on a shelf. "The ace card was driven right into the wall—where it stuck," remembered twelve-year-old Billy Joe Nava.

During the 1970 tornado, a piece of glass from the hog house was driven into a tree on the Hylands' Iowa farm (below).

The power of tornadoes also has made deep impressions on the minds of people. An 1861 tornado that struck Camanche, Iowa was witnessed by a farmer named Benjamin F. Gue. Gue, later lieutenant governor of Iowa, wrote this description:

> Suddenly the funnel rose into the air and I could see falling to the earth tree tops, rails, boards, posts, and every conceivable broken fragment of wrecked buildings . . . . It was an awe-inspiring sight. . . . The cloud of inky blackness settled down to the earth again in the distance, sweeping on with a mighty power, glowing with a thousand forked tongues of lightning as the very earth seemed to tremble beneath the incessant roar of thunder. No pen or tongue can convey to the mind a true picture of the frightful sights and sounds . . . of that irresistible tornado.

One hundred and twenty years later, newspaperman Dennis Spruill sat in his office and remembered how he felt when the Wichita Falls tornado almost sucked him out of his house: "I've never felt anything like the power of that tornado," he said. "I felt it could overcome any obstacle I could think of. I could feel and sense its power all around me. I can't even put into words the feeling of its great power. I've never had to describe something like that before. It was that ultimate phenomenon of nature we've named a tornado."

6/PREDICTING AND PREPARING

Charles Dudley Warner once wrote that "Everybody talks about the weather, but nobody does anything about it." This is only partly true of tornadoes. No one has figured out a way to keep them from forming. But the United States has a system to warn people of tornadoes.

The National Weather Service has a special office in Kansas City, Missouri. This office is called the National Severe Storms Forecast Center. Meteorologists there watch for conditions across the country that may create tornadoes.

You may wonder how meteorologists in Kansas City can predict tornadoes many hundreds of miles away. The scientists have many tools to help them:

- *Weather satellites* provide an overhead view of the country's weather. Orbiting thousands of miles above the earth, the satellites take pictures of cloud formations. These pictures are sent to the center in Kansas City. Tornadoes can't be spotted on the satellite pictures. But thunderstorms that may contain tornadoes can be seen.

Below: A morning map meeting at the National Severe Storms Forecast Center in Kansas City, Missouri.

This radar antenna inside a protective dome (above) detects precipitation. Weather balloons (above right) carry upper-air measuring instruments. Right: A radar console at the National Severe Storms Laboratory.

- The *radar network* maintained by the National Weather Service is a second important tool. The radar signals reflect off raindrops and hail high up in the sky, thereby showing places where there are storms. Tornadoes can develop in such places. The radar reports are sent by teletype and computer to the National Severe Storms Forecast Center. Once in a while a tornado can actually be seen on radar. It shows up as a hook-shaped pattern.
- *Hourly observations* made at the hundreds of weather stations across the country are a third important tool. The reports are sent by teletype and computer to the National Severe Storms Forecast Center. These reports sometimes indicate that conditions are right for tornadoes.

Frederick Ostby, Director of the National Severe Storms Forecast Center

What if the scientists at the National Severe Storms Forecast Center think that tornadoes may form over a certain area?

"We issue what is called a *tornado watch*," explained Frederick Ostby, the director of the center. A tornado watch does not necessarily mean that tornadoes have been spotted. It means that conditions are right for the formation of tornadoes and that people should watch the sky. "A tornado watch usually is for a large area — 25,000 square miles or so," Ostby explained. "We try to give the watch two to six hours before tornadoes form."

Tornado watch information is sent to local weather stations and then broadcast on radio and television. The following tornado watch information was sent out by the National Severe Storms Forecast Center on April 10, 1981:

THE NATIONAL SEVERE STORMS FORECAST CENTER HAS ISSUED A TORNADO WATCH FOR A LARGE PART OF WEST CENTRAL ILLINOIS, SOUTH CENTRAL AND SOUTHEASTERN IOWA, AND A SMALL PART OF NORTHERN MISSOURI FROM 2:00 P.M. CENTRAL STANDARD TIME UNTIL 8:00 P.M. THIS FRIDAY AFTERNOON AND EVENING. TORNADOES, LARGE HAIL, AND DAMAGING THUNDERSTORM WINDS ARE POSSIBLE IN THESE AREAS... REMEMBER, A TORNADO WATCH MEANS CONDITIONS ARE FAVORABLE FOR TORNADOES AND SEVERE THUNDERSTORMS IN AND CLOSE TO THE WATCH AREA. PERSONS IN THESE AREAS SHOULD BE ON THE LOOKOUT FOR THREATENING WEATHER CONDITIONS AND LISTEN FOR LATER STATEMENTS AND POSSIBLE WARNINGS.

People in Illinois, Iowa, and Missouri who were watching television or listening to the radio heard the above tornado watch statement.

Don't get upset if you ever hear that there's a tornado watch. A huge area may be involved—perhaps a whole state. In that whole area there may be only one or two tornadoes— or perhaps none at all. But if you do hear that a tornado watch is in effect, do watch television. What you're waiting for is a possible *tornado warning*. Tornado warnings—issued by individual weather offices—mean that a tornado has actually been spotted by human eye or radar.

The following tornado warning was given just before the tornado struck Vernon, Texas in 1979. It was released by the National Weather Service office in Wichita Falls, Texas and was broadcast on radio and television on the afternoon of April 10, 1979:

THE NATIONAL WEATHER SERVICE HAS ISSUED A TORNADO WARNING EFFECTIVE UNTIL 4:30 P.M. CST FOR WILBARGER

COUNTY OF TEXAS INCLUDING THE CITY OF VERNON. AT
3:28 P.M. A TORNADO WAS REPORTED BY BOTH THE TEXAS
HIGHWAY DEPARTMENT AND THE VERNON POLICE
DEPARTMENT TO BE LOCATED ALONG THE PEASE RIVER
NEAR THE RAYLAND COMMUNITY JUST WEST OF LOCKETT
MOVING TOWARD THE NORTHEAST. DEBRIS WAS REPORTED
IN THE RAYLAND AREA ALTHOUGH NO REPORTS OF
INJURIES WERE RECEIVED. PERSONS ALONG THE PEASE
RIVER BETWEEN RAYLAND AND THE CITY OF VERNON
SHOULD SEEK A PLACE OF SAFETY IMMEDIATELY.

Not everyone will be watching television or listening to the
radio to hear the tornado warning. Therefore, many
communities sound horns or sirens when a tornado warning
is given.

When you hear the tornado sirens—or a tornado warning
for your community on television—it's time to take action.
Remember, the *warning* means that a tornado has actually
been spotted. There are simple steps you can take to protect
yourself and your family from a possible tornado. The
National Weather Service gives this advice for times of
tornado warnings:

- If you're at home when the tornado warning is given, go down
  into your basement or cellar. If your house doesn't have a
  basement or cellar, go into a closet or bathroom near the
  middle of the house. The hiding place you choose is very
  important. The most protected areas of your house will best
  protect you.

- Once in your hiding place, get under a staircase, a table, a
  desk, or some other sturdy piece of furniture. Also, try to cover
  your head with pillows, mattresses, blankets, or towels. Your
  head should be protected in case glass or wood is sent flying.
  Stay away from windows!

- In schools, hospitals, and factories there are usually places
  that have been designated as shelter areas. In a school, the
  safest place is usually an inside hallway on the lowest floor. If
  a tornado is coming, a teacher will probably say something
  like: "Everybody crouch down on your elbows and knees!

The lightning associated with a thunderstorm or a tornado can be very beautiful, but it is also very dangerous.

Hands over the back of your head!" Listen to the instructions and follow them.

- If you're in school when a tornado warning is given, be sure to stay away from big rooms such as the cafeteria, auditorium, and gym. Such big rooms have ceilings that may cave in.

- If you're outside on the streets of your town when a tornado warning is given, get off the street. Go into a building. Even if there's no tornado, you don't want to be out in a thunderstorm.

- Should you be in a car when a tornado warning is given, get out of it. As you've learned, a car is one of the most dangerous places to be during a tornado. If you have time, get inside a building. If the tornado is approaching and there is no building nearby, get out of the car, lie down in a ditch or on the ground, and protect your head.

- If you live in a mobile home, leave it quickly. Like cars, mobile homes are dangerous places to be when a tornado strikes. They are often turned over or picked up and flung long distances.

- Also very important—try to decide on a tornado hiding place long *before* one strikes. Your family might discuss the best hiding place together. People who have plans don't lose time looking for a hiding place when the tornado sirens are sounded.

If you are in a car when you hear a tornado warning, get out of the car and go into a building or lie down in a ditch and protect your head (above). If you are at home, go down into the basement or into a closet or bathroom in the middle of the house. Get under a sturdy piece of furniture (below) or a staircase (left) and cover your head with pillows or a mattress.

Mobile homes are among the most dangerous places to be when a
tornado strikes. They are often demolished, turned over, or flung
long distances. Tornadoes that ripped through these two trailer
parks left nothing in their wake except concrete foundations and debris.

After reading about tornadoes, you might be afraid that one will hit you. Chances are that your home will never be struck by a tornado. Even if your community's tornado sirens are sounded, the twister may strike several miles away or not even touch down. In all your life you'll probably never even *see* a tornado in the distance. But if you do, you should know what course of action to take.

The United States tornado warning system has saved many lives. In the 1930s—before the National Severe Storms Forecast Center was established—about two hundred people a year were killed by tornadoes in the United States. In the 1970s, only about a hundred people a year died in tornadoes. This is an even greater saving of lives than it sounds. The population of the United States just about doubled between the 1930s and the 1970s, and the cities grew much larger. So tornadoes had bigger targets.

Here is an example of how the tornado warning system saved a large number of lives:

At 3:00 P.M. on May 12, 1980, the National Severe Storms Forecast Center issued a tornado watch for a large area that included Sedalia, Missouri. At 5:00 P.M., shortly after a tornado had been spotted, the National Weather Service office in Columbia, Missouri issued a tornado warning for the Sedalia area. At 5:02 P.M., Sedalia's tornado sirens were sounded. In a Sedalia trailer park, more than 100 people in 64 mobile homes heard the sirens. They left their mobile homes and went into the basement of the park manager's home. The tornado slammed into Sedalia at 5:14 P.M. Almost all the mobile homes were smashed. But because the people had taken shelter in the basement of a house, they survived.

"We think we've done a good job in reducing the death toll from tornadoes," says Frederick Ostby, director of the

Above: This tornado struck Union City, Oklahoma on May 23, 1973.
Below: This July 12, 1971 tornado was photographed by Mrs. Everett White when it was about a mile away from her Mitchell, Iowa home.

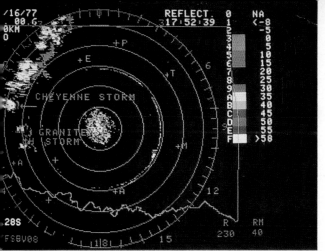

Doppler radar can measure wind speeds within a thunderstorm and show the presence of rotating winds. It can "see" a storm that is capable of producing a tornado about twenty minutes before the actual tornado can be seen on the ground. Below left: A Doppler radar antenna. Left and below: Color Doppler radar displays of tornadic storms.

National Severe Storms Forecast Center. "We hope to do an even better job in the future.

"Doppler radar is one of the technological advances that will help us. Doppler radar can measure wind speeds within a thunderstorm and show the presence of rotating winds. By 1990, we expect a network of Doppler radar to replace existing radar. It will allow us to detect tornadoes more positively before they touch ground."

While scientists are working on new ways to detect tornadoes, you can do something to protect yourself and your family from the greatest winds on earth. Make a plan and follow it if a tornado warning is given.

Above: A tornado approaches a harbor.
Below: This tornado was nearing an Andrews, Texas school yard in 1965.

Glossary

Clockwise Circular motion in the same direction as the hands of a clock

Counterclockwise Circular motion in the opposite direction from the hands of a clock

Disaster A sudden, destructive event that causes great damage and loss

Doppler radar An instrument that can measure wind speeds within a thunderstorm and show the presence of rotating winds

Front The boundary between two different kinds of air, such as warm, moist southern air and cold, dry northern air

Funnel A whirling tornado cloud shaped like a hollow cone with a tube extending down from the smaller end

Hurricane A huge, powerful windstorm that whirls in a circular motion and covers thousands of square miles; it is much larger than a tornado, but its winds are not as strong

Meteorologist A weather scientist

Radar An instrument that can detect and locate distant objects by means of reflected radio waves

Rotate Spin

Storm cellar A cellar used for protection from windstorms or tornadoes

Thunderstorm A violent storm accompanied by thunder and lightning that often develops in the United States when warm, moist air from the south rises to meet cold, dry air from the north

Tornado A violently whirling column of air that descends from a thundercloud system and touches the ground; it is the most powerful and destructive storm on earth

"Tornado Alley" A wide north-south band roughly in the middle of the United States within which most tornadoes occur

Tornado warning A message from a local weather office stating that a tornado has been sighted nearby and that all persons in the area should seek a place of safety immediately

Tornado watch A message from a local weather office stating that conditions are favorable for tornadoes and severe thunderstorms in the watch area; all persons in the area should be aware of the danger and listen for a possible tornado warning

Vortex The inside of a tornado

Waterspout A tornado that touches down on a lake or an ocean and sucks up water into its swirling winds

Weather balloon A balloon that carries instruments aloft to measure the temperature, moisture, and pressure characteristics in the upper air

Weather satellite An instrument that orbits thousands of miles above the earth and takes pictures of cloud formations which are relayed to weather stations on the ground

Index

Photo Credits

LEO AINSWORTH PHOTOGRAPH, COURTESY NATIONAL SEVERE STORMS LABORATORY,
   NOAA—Cover, page 26
NATIONAL SEVERE STORMS LABORATORY, NOAA-Pages 2, 50, 54, 58 (top), 59
SATELLITE FIELD SERVICES STATION, NOAA—Page 4
W.H. HALL-Pages 7 (top), 15, 16, 17
WICHITA FALLS TIMES AND RECORD NEWS-Pages 7 (bottom),8, 10, 18
UPI-Pages 20, 24, 25, 27, 31, 32, 33, 36, 43, 44, 56, 60
NOAA (NATIONAL OCEANIC AND ATMOSPHERIC ADMINISTRATION)-Pages 21, 23
FLINT JOURNAL PHOTO-Pages 38, 39
SIGURD AND LOUISE HYLAND-Pages 46, 47
NATIONAL SEVERE STORMS FORECAST CENTER, NOAA-Pages 49, 51
MRS. EVERETT WHITE-Page 58 (bottom)
LEN MEENTS (ART)-Pages 30, 41, 55

COVER PHOTOGRAPH—A tornado approaches Enid, Oklahoma

About the author

Dennis Fradin attended Northwestern University on a partial creative writing scholarship and graduated in 1967. He has published stories and articles in such places as *Ingenue, The Saturday Evening Post, Scholastic, Chicago, Oui,* and *National Humane Review.* His previous books include the Young People's Stories of Our States series for Childrens Press and *Bad Luck Tony* for Prentice-Hall. He is married and the father of three children.

About the artist

Len Meents studied painting and drawing at Southern Illinois University and after graduation in 1969 he moved to Chicago. Mr. Meents works full time as a painter and illustrator. He and his wife and child currently make their home in LaGrange, Illinois.